Presented to:

By:

Date:

Occasion:

Warner Books, Inc., 1271 Avenue of the Americas, New York, NY 10020

Visit our website at www.twbookmark.com

WARNER *Faith* A Division of AOL Time Warner Book Group
The Warner Faith name and logo are registered trademarks of Warner Books, Inc.

Printed in the United States of America

First Printing: May 2003
10 9 8 7 6 5 4 3 2 1

ISBN: 0-446-53249-5
LCCN: 2003101819

THE POWER
OF FORGIVENESS

Keep Your Heart Free

JOYCE MEYER

WARNER
Faith

Contents

WHY WE
MUST
FORGIVE

🥀

Jesus taught us that we are to forgive those who hurt us, to pray for those who despitefully use us, and to bless those who curse us. That is hard. But there is something harder—being full of hatred, bitterness, and resentment.

GOD'S WORD FOR YOU

The Spirit of the Lord God is upon me, because the Lord has anointed and qualified me to preach the Gospel of good tidings to the meek, the poor, and afflicted; He has sent me to bind up and heal the brokenhearted, to proclaim liberty to the [physical and spiritual] captives and the opening of the prison and of the eyes to those who are bound . . .

ISAIAH 61:1

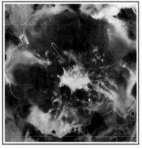

o n e

WHY WE MUST FORGIVE

ave you been hurt? Misused? Abused? Treated wrongly or improperly? Rejected? Has it affected your emotional state? Do you really want to be healed? Do you really want to get well? Will you forgive?

I believe that most people are abused in one way or another during their lifetime. It may come in the form of physical, verbal, emotional, or sexual abuse. Whatever form it takes, abuse causes a root of rejection, which is a devastating problem in our day.

I know all too much about this. I was sexually, physically, verbally, and emotionally abused from the time I can remember until I left home at the age of eighteen. I have been rejected, abandoned, betrayed, and divorced. I know what it means to hurt . . . and I thank God that He has shown me how to recover.

Wounded emotions can become a prison that locks us into our pain and keeps others out. Perhaps you are in the condition in life where I was, an emotional prisoner. It's a bitter, resentful, angry prison cell, and forgiveness is the key that unlocks the door that holds us there. How long have you been there? Do you want to be free of it?

Jesus came to open prison doors and to set the captives free! He wants to heal you. Jesus is willing; are you?

9

GOD'S WORD FOR YOU

There was a certain man there who had suffered with a deep-seated and lingering disorder for thirty-eight years.

When Jesus noticed him lying there [helpless], knowing that he had already been a long time in that condition, He said to him, Do you want to become well? [Are you really in earnest about getting well?]

JOHN 5:5–6

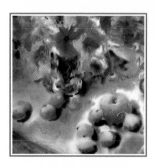

A QUESTION FOR THE HEART

For many, many years, "Why me, God?" was the cry of my heart, and it filled my thoughts and affected my attitude daily. I lived in the wilderness of self-pity, and it was a problem for me, my family, and the plan of God for my life. My troubled mind caused me to have a chip on my shoulder and to expect everyone else to fix my problem. I felt as though I was due something for the way I had been treated, but I was looking to people to pay me back when I should have been looking to God.

When Jesus addressed His question to the man who had been lying by the pool of Bethesda for thirty-eight years, He knew that self-pity would not deliver this man. "Do you want to become well?" are words of compassion to anyone who is trapped in an emotional prison and who has learned to function with their problem. They are words directed to the heart.

Gaining freedom from hurts and emotional bondages is not easy. I know. It will provoke feelings and emotions that have been "stuffed" rather than faced and dealt with. It may involve very real pain, but to be free and cleansed by the power of forgiveness is the only way to ever be fully well again.

God told me I could be pitiful or powerful, but I could not be both. I had to give up the self-pity to be free.

GOD'S WORD FOR YOU

In Him we have redemption (deliverance and salvation) through His blood, the remission (forgiveness) of our offenses (shortcomings and trespasses), in accordance with the riches and the generosity of His gracious favor,

Which He lavished upon us in every kind of wisdom and understanding (practical insight and prudence) . . .

EPHESIANS 1:7–8

PERSONAL SIN

To forgive those who have hurt us in the past is one of the ways we break the bondage of an emotional prison. But for many of us, dealing with our personal sin consciousness can also be a huge problem. The good news is that it doesn't have to be.

For a host of reasons that we will consider in this book, you may struggle with your sins in a way that you don't see in other believers' lives. When you sin or fail in any way, even when you make a mistake or display a weakness, you feel trapped there. You wonder if God is angry at you, and it's easy to doubt that He loves you. And you feel that you need to somehow atone for what you've done.

You know all the words about redemption and remission of our sins, and how God puts our sins away from Him as far as the east is from the west. But the faith to receive the gift of God's forgiveness doesn't seem to catch hold and work for you as it does for others.

I know about it. As a new believer, I would beg God's forgiveness for all my past sins every night. I wondered if I would ever find the peace I sought.

One evening as I prayed, I heard God say, "I forgave you the first time you asked, but you have not received My gift because you have not forgiven yourself."

GOD'S WORD FOR YOU

Asked by the Pharisees when the kingdom of God would come, He replied to them by saying, The kingdom of God does not come with signs to be observed or with visible display,

Nor will people say, Look! Here [it is]! or, See, [it is] there! For behold, the kingdom of God is within you [in your hearts] and among you [surrounding you].

LUKE 17:20–21

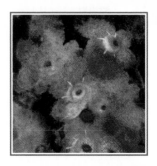

WHAT'S WRONG WITH ME?

For years in my Christian life I walked around with the nagging thought, *What's wrong with me?* Is that a question that troubles you as well?

I tried to do all the right things. My husband was an elder in the church, and I was on the evangelism committee and the church board. Our children went to parochial school. We didn't miss a church service, and I did everything I was told I should do to become spiritual. I tried and tried and tried, and yet it seemed that I just could not keep myself from making mistakes. I tried to earn righteousness by being good through the works of the flesh. And I ended up worn out, burned out, frustrated, and miserable.

It never occurred to me that I was suffering from years of abuse and rejection I had gone through. I thought that was all behind me. It was true that I was no longer being sexually abused, but it was all recorded in my emotions and my mind. I still had the effects of it, and I still acted them out. I needed to be healed emotionally, and I needed to forgive. I did not know the power of the kingdom of God within me.

I lived out of my own mind, will, and emotions, which were all damaged. Jesus had paid the price for my total deliverance, but I had no idea how to receive His gracious gift.

GOD'S WORD FOR YOU

You will fully recognize them by their fruits. Do people pick grapes from thorns, or figs from thistles?

Even so, every healthy (sound) tree bears good fruit [worthy of admiration], but the sickly (decaying, worthless) tree bears bad (worthless) fruit.

A good (healthy) tree cannot bear bad (worthless) fruit, nor can a bad (diseased) tree bear excellent fruit [worthy of admiration].

Every tree that does not bear good fruit is cut down and cast into the fire.

Therefore, you will fully know them by their fruits.

MATTHEW 7:16–20

By Your Fruit

The first thing to realize is that the fruit in our lives (our behavior) comes from somewhere. A person who is angry is that way for a reason. His behavior is the bad fruit of a bad tree with bad roots. It is important that we take a close and honest look at our fruit as well as our roots.

In my own life, there was a lot of bad fruit. I experienced regular bouts of depression, negativism, self-pity, quick temper, and the chip-on-the-shoulder syndrome. I had a controlling, domineering spirit. I was harsh, hard, rigid, legalistic, and judgmental. I held grudges and was fearful.

I worked hard at trying to correct it. Yet it seemed that no matter what kind of bad behavior I tried to get rid of, two or three others popped up somewhere else. It was like dandelions. I was not getting to the hidden root of the problem, and it would not die.

If this scenario sounds familiar to you, it may be that you have unresolved issues in your life that need to be searched out and removed so that everything can be made fresh and new. Don't run away. If God can change me, He certainly can change you.

Rotten fruit comes from rotten roots;
good fruit comes from good roots.

GOD'S WORD FOR YOU

For if you forgive people their trespasses [their reckless and willful sins, leaving them, letting them go, and giving up resentment], your heavenly Father will also forgive you.

But if you do not forgive others their trespasses [their reckless and willful sins, leaving them, letting them go, and giving up resentment], neither will your Father forgive you your trespasses.

MATTHEW 6:14–15

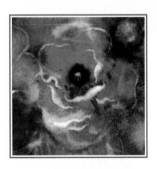

PROBLEMS PEOPLE MANIFEST

The fruit of unforgiveness creates a heart condition that is very dangerous, because the Bible tells us plainly that if we will not forgive other people, then God cannot forgive us. If we cannot forgive others, our faith doesn't work, and that has serious consequences.

Some people experience feelings of unworthiness. They have a shame-based self-hatred, a sense of self-rejection, and an inner voice that tells them they are no good, that something is wrong with them.

Other people become perfectionists. They are always trying to prove their worth and gain love and acceptance through performance. These people always struggle to do a little bit better in the hope that someone will love and accept them more.

Still others are supersensitive. Are you "touchy"? Would you like to be delivered from supersensitivity? If so, you need to face the fact that the problem is not with those who offend and hurt you, it is with you and your heart condition. Being secure will heal you of this.

Hatred, bitterness, resentment, loneliness, and addictions can be added to the list of bad fruit.

God has the marvelous ability to love us in the midst of our imperfections, and He wants to heal us. But in order for Him to do so, we must be willing to be helped.

GOD'S WORD FOR YOU

Go through, go through the gates! Prepare the way for the people. Cast up, cast up the highway! Gather out the stones. Lift up a standard or ensign over and for the peoples.

Behold, the Lord has proclaimed to the end of the earth: Say to the Daughter of Zion, Behold, your salvation comes [in the person of the Lord]; behold, His reward is with Him, and His work and recompense before Him.

And they shall call them the Holy People, the Redeemed of the Lord; and you shall be called Sought Out, a City Not Forsaken.

ISAIAH 62:10–12

PRETENDING

I was so miserable and unhappy. Yet, like so many people, I pretended that everything was fine. We human beings pretend for the benefit of others, not wanting them to know about our misery, but we also pretend for ourselves so that we do not have to face and deal with difficult issues.

Perhaps this describes you? I was one person on the inside and another on the outside. I pretended to be very confident, and in some ways I was. Still, I had very low self-esteem, and my so-called confidence was not really based on who I was in Christ. It was based on the approval of others, on my appearance and accomplishments, and on other external factors. Strip away the superficial exterior, and I was scared stiff. I was confused and full of inner turmoil.

The day came when I realized I had to face the truth and stop pretending. I don't think I ever realized just how miserable I was until I had spent some time in the Word of God and had begun to experience some emotional healing. If a person has never known true happiness, as was true of my life, how can he know what he is missing?

God will be your reward, and He will recompense you for what you have lost and what is missing.

GOD'S WORD FOR YOU

And we know (understand, recognize, are conscious of, by observation and by experience) and believe (adhere to and put faith in and rely on) the love God cherishes for us. God is love, and he who dwells and continues in love dwells and continues in God, and God dwells and continues in him.

In this [union and communion with Him] love is brought to completion and attains perfection with us, that we may have confidence for the day of judgment [with assurance and boldness to face Him], because as He is, so are we in this world.

There is no fear in love [dread does not exist], but full-grown (complete, perfect) love turns fear out of doors and expels every trace of terror! For fear brings with it the thought of punishment, and [so] he who is afraid has not reached the full maturity of love [is not yet grown into love's complete perfection].

We love Him, because He first loved us.

1 JOHN 4:16–19

STARVED FOR LOVE

We are created by God for love. Loving and being loved are what make life worth living. It gives life purpose and meaning. But if we have allowed sin and unforgiveness and the past to separate us from His love, it will leave us love-starved and unhappy.

Many people cannot maintain healthy, lasting relationships because either they don't know how to receive love or they place an unbalanced demand on others to give them what only God can give. The resulting frustration often leads to the ruin of marriages and the suffocation of friendships.

The Bible teaches us that God loves perfectly or unconditionally. His perfect love for us is not based on our perfection. It is not based on anything except Himself. God is Love (1 John 4:8). Love is Who He is. God always loves, but we often stop receiving His love.

God dealt with me for one solid year to get me to understand that He loves me unconditionally, not conditionally. I was unable to put my faith in His love because I was trapped in my unworthiness.

The day of liberation finally came for me.
God graciously revealed to me, through the Holy Spirit,
His love for me personally. That single revelation
changed my entire life and walk with Him.

GOD'S WORD FOR YOU

I am the Door; anyone who enters in through Me will be saved (will live). He will come in and he will go out [freely], and will find pasture.

The thief comes only in order to steal and kill and destroy. I came that they may have and enjoy life, and have it in abundance (to the full, till it overflows).

I am the Good Shepherd. The Good Shepherd risks and lays down His [own] life for the sheep.

JOHN 10:9–11

WALLS OF PROTECTION

After we have been hurt or felt the pain from rejection, it is our natural reaction to build elaborate defense systems of walls around our lives to protect our emotions from the same happening again. We put up an invisible (but real) wall between us and anyone who might be able to hurt us.

You see, Satan works in many different ways to steal your freedom and joy. These two go together! If Satan steals your freedom, he will also steal your joy. You will end up living in a little box, always trying to do what you think will be acceptable to everybody else . . . never being led by the Holy Spirit within you.

Self-made walls of protection never work. No one totally escapes rejection from others. Only God can build walls of protection around our lives, and it only happens by faith in His protection. We must allow the Holy Spirit to tear down the wrong walls so He can activate the protection of God that became available to us through salvation.

If you find yourself walled into your own little world, it's time to come out of your house and say, "I'm the King's kid! I'm going to walk without my walls! I'm believing God for a new start today! I will forgive."

RECEIVING FORGIVENESS

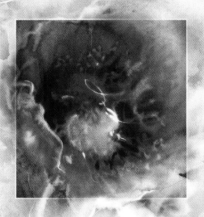

*Receiving forgiveness for past mistakes
and sins, and forgiving others for their
mistakes and sins, are two of the most
important and powerful factors in healing
our emotions and discovering
our freedom in Christ.*

GOD'S WORD FOR YOU

Jesus said to him, I am the Way and the Truth and the Life; no one comes to the Father except by (through) Me.

JOHN 14:6

But be doers of the Word [obey the message], and not merely listeners to it, betraying yourselves [into deception by reasoning contrary to the Truth].

JAMES 1:22

t w o

RECEIVING FORGIVENESS

any people are hurting so badly, and they are crying out for help. The *problem* is, they are not willing to receive the help they need from God.

The *truth* is, no matter how much we may want or need help, we are never going to receive it until we are willing to do things God's way. It is amazing how many times we want help, but we want it *our* way.

In John 14:6, what Jesus meant when He said, "I am the Way," is that He has a certain way of doing things, and if we will submit to *His* way, everything will work out for us.

Matthew 6:14–15 says that if we forgive men when they sin against us, our heavenly Father will also forgive us. If we do not forgive men their sins, our heavenly Father will not forgive ours.

To receive from God what He has promised us in His Word, we must obey the Word, whether or not it is hard to act on it. Yes, we must receive the Word, but then we must become doers of the Word. We are not to wait to act according to our feelings.

God's way works! Forgiveness is a gift given to those who do not and will never deserve it. The power of forgiveness is the only way to freedom.

If we will do what we can, God will do what we can't.

GOD'S WORD FOR YOU

So Jesus said to those Jews who had believed in Him, If you abide in My word [hold fast to My teachings and live in accordance with them], you are truly My disciples.

And you will know the Truth, and the Truth will set you free.

JOHN 8:31–32

And when He comes, He will convict and convince the world and bring demonstration to it about sin and about righteousness (uprightness of heart and right standing with God) and about judgment:

About sin, because they do not believe in Me [trust in, rely on, and adhere to Me];

About righteousness (uprightness of heart and right standing with God), because I go to My Father, and you will see Me no longer . . .

JOHN 16:8–10

Know the Truth

The Holy Spirit leads us through different steps to experience freedom in our lives. He guided me through the process while healing my emotions, which were damaged from years of abuse. I believe the Holy Spirit will guide you too as you seek to find victory and restoration of your broken spirit.

First, you must acknowledge the truth. You cannot be set free if you are living in denial. You cannot pretend either that certain negative things did not happen to you, or that you have not been influenced by them or reacted in response to them. Don't keep unforgiveness hidden away in a dark corner.

Ask the Holy Spirit to lead and guide you in this process. He convicts us of sin by exposing us to the truth that sets us free, but He never condemns us. He brings conviction so that we can see our errors, admit them, be truly sorry, repent, and receive forgiveness and cleansing in the precious blood of Jesus. The Holy Spirit has the power to break any bondage you may have, and He will enable you to walk free from what has been a sin in your life.

It is so wonderful to have Jesus as a friend, because He already knows everything about you. Why hide from Him? Come to Him and know you are loved and accepted no matter what is on your heart.

GOD'S WORD FOR YOU

Is anyone among you sick? He should call in the church elders (the spiritual guides). And they should pray over him, anointing him with oil in the Lord's name.

And the prayer [that is] of faith will save him who is sick, and the Lord will restore him; and if he has committed sins, he will be forgiven.

Confess to one another therefore your faults (your slips, your false steps, your offenses, your sins) and pray [also] for one another, that you may be healed and restored [to a spiritual tone of mind and heart]. The earnest (heartfelt, continued) prayer of a righteous man makes tremendous power available [dynamic in its working].

JAMES 5:14–16

CONFESS YOUR FAULTS

It is possible that you should consider putting James 5:16 into action. I think there is a place for eventually sharing with someone else if you are being tormented by your past sins. Being poisoned inwardly keeps you from getting well—physically, mentally, spiritually, or emotionally. There is something powerful about verbalizing it to another person that does wonders for us. That person can agree with you concerning your forgiveness and can even pray for you to be forgiven.

Once exposed to the light, things hidden in the dark lose their power. People hide things because of fear of what others would think if they knew. Numerous people have come to me for prayer, confiding in me, "I've never told this to anyone, but I feel I need to get it out of my system." Often they weep, and then a desperately needed release would come.

Use wisdom in whom you choose as a confidant. Ask God to lead you to a mature believer whom you can trust. It should be someone who is not going to be burdened down or harmed by what you share or use it to hurt you or make you feel worse about yourself.

The practice of confessing our faults to one another and receiving prayer is a powerful tool to help break bondages.

GOD'S WORD FOR YOU

Behold, You desire truth in the inner being; make me therefore to know wisdom in my inmost heart.

PSALM 51:6

TELL YOURSELF THE TRUTH

God wants us to face the truth in our inmost being, then confess it in an appropriate manner to the right person. Sometimes the person who needs to hear the truth the most is us.

When people come to me for help in this area, I often tell them, "Go and look at yourself in the mirror and confess the problem to yourself."

If, for instance, your problem is that your parents did not love you as a child and you are resentful and bitter, face the facts as a reality once and for all. Look at yourself in the mirror and say, "My parents did not love me, and perhaps they never will."

Don't be one of those people who spend your life trying to get something you will never have. If you have let the fact that you were unloved ruin your life thus far, don't let it claim the rest of your life. Do what David did. Confess to yourself: "Although my father and my mother have forsaken me, yet the Lord will take me up [adopt me as His child]" (Psalm 27:10).

Whatever the problem may be that is bothering you, face it, consider confessing it to a trusted confidant, then admit it to yourself in your inmost being.

Admitting the truth causes the past to lose its grip on us.

GOD'S WORD FOR YOU

I, even I, am He Who blots out and cancels your transgressions, for My own sake, and I will not remember your sins.

ISAIAH 43:25

For as the heavens are high above the earth, so great are His mercy and loving-kindness toward those who reverently and worshipfully fear Him.

As far as the east is from the west, so far has He removed our transgressions from us.

As a father loves and pities his children, so the Lord loves and pities those who fear Him [with reverence, worship, and awe].

PSALM 103:11–13

RECEIVE YOUR FORGIVENESS

No matter what your problem or how bad you feel about yourself as a result of it, take this truth into your heart: God loves you. Jesus Christ gave His life that you might be forgiven, and He has given you a new life. God has given you a new family and new friends to love and accept and appreciate and support you. You are going to make it because of the One Who lives inside you and cares for you.

Confess to God whatever it is that stands between Him and you as sin. No matter what you may have done, say, "Lord, I did it, and it is a marvel to me to realize that I can stand here and look myself in the eye. But I can do so because I know that, even though what I did was wrong, You have put my sins as far away from me as the east is from the west, and You remember them no more!"

Once you have confessed your sins and asked for God's forgiveness, if you continue to drag them up to Him every time you go to Him in prayer, you are reminding Him of something He has not only *forgiven* but also actually *forgotten*.

From this moment, stop punishing yourself for something that no longer exists.

GOD'S WORD FOR YOU

In Him we have redemption (deliverance and salvation) through His blood, the remission (forgiveness) of our offenses (shortcomings and trespasses), in accordance with the riches and the generosity of His gracious favor . . .

EPHESIANS 1:7

You were bought with a price [purchased with a preciousness and paid for, made His own]. So then, honor God and bring glory to Him in your body.

1 CORINTHIANS 6:20

PURCHASED BY JESUS' BLOOD

Say aloud to yourself, "I was bought and cleansed from sin with a price; purchased with a preciousness; paid for and made God's own."

We are delivered from sin and all the "death" it brings with it. Worry, anxiety, and fear are forms of death. Strife, bitterness, resentment, and unforgiveness are forms of death. The blood of Jesus is the only antidote for death.

Jesus' blood is precious before the Father and should be precious to us. A precious thing is something we protect, something we are careful with, something we don't want to part with. The blood of Jesus is precious, and it should be honored and respected.

The blood of Jesus cleanses us from sin and will continuously cleanse us (1 John 1:9). His blood is like a powerful cleansing agent. Just as our blood works to keep our bodies cleansed of all poison, the blood of Jesus continuously cleanses us from sin in all its forms and manifestations.

Repentance releases the power of the blood of Jesus in your behalf. Let the Lord "wash" you in the blood. Release your faith in the blood of Jesus.

GOD'S WORD FOR YOU

Therefore, [there is] now no condemnation (no adjudging guilty of wrong) for those who are in Christ Jesus, who live [and] walk not after the dictates of the flesh, but after the dictates of the Spirit.

ROMANS 8:1

GUILT AND CONDEMNATION

One of the major problems for many believers is the recurrence of feeling guilty and condemned for past sins that they have received forgiveness for. Satan's great delight is to make us feel bad about ourselves, and one way to do that is by telling us our forgiveness wasn't complete.

The Bible teaches that through the blood of Jesus we have complete forgiveness and total freedom from condemnation. We don't need to add our guilt to His sacrifice upon the cross. He is more than enough.

If the devil tries to bring that sin to your mind again in the form of guilt and condemnation, declare to him: "I was forgiven for that sin! It has been taken care of; therefore, I take no care for it." You will find that speaking aloud is often helpful to you because by doing so you are declaring your stand on the Word of God. Declare to the principalities and powers that Christ has set you free.

Don't just sit and listen to the devil's accusations and lies. Learn to talk back to him with the truth. Begin to see yourself as the righteousness of God in Christ Jesus.

GOD'S WORD FOR YOU

Therefore I will not restrain my mouth; I will speak in the anguish of my spirit, I will complain in the bitterness of my soul [O Lord]!

JOB 7:11

FORGIVING GOD

Many people have problems of unforgiveness toward God. Those who have never experienced that feeling may not understand it. But those who have know what it is to feel animosity toward God because they blame Him for cheating them out of something important in their lives. Things have not worked out the way they had planned. They figure that God could have changed things if He had wanted to, but since He didn't, they feel disappointed and blame Him for their situation.

If you are holding on to this attitude, you know it is impossible to have fellowship with someone you are mad at. If so, the only answer is to forgive God. Of course, God does not need to be forgiven! But such heart honesty can break the bondage and restore the fellowship that has been broken with the Lord.

Often we think if we just knew *why* certain things happened to us, we would be satisfied. I believe God tells us only what we really need to know, what we are prepared to handle, and what will not harm us, but will, in fact, help us. We must learn to trust God and not try to figure out everything in life.

There must come a time when we stop living in the past and asking why. Instead, we must learn to let God turn our scars into stars.

GOD'S WORD FOR YOU

And this is the message [the message of promise] which we have heard from Him and now are reporting to you: God is Light, and there is no darkness in Him at all [no, not in any way].

[So] if we say we are partakers together and enjoy fellowship with Him when we live and move and are walking about in darkness, we are [both] speaking falsely and do not live and practice the Truth [which the Gospel presents].

1 JOHN 1:5–6

OPENING UP TO GOD

The power of forgiveness frees us from all guilt and condemnation and allows us to come out of the darkness into the light of God (1 John 1:5–6). So often in the past we tried to hide things by burying them deep inside our own darkness. But in God there is no darkness at all. So when we allow Him full entrance into our hearts and minds, there is no darkness.

I am so glad that God fills every room of my heart with His light. There are no places in my heart that I know of that are blocked off from Him and the light that comes from His presence.

We must allow the Lord to come into the dark recesses of the heart and fill them with His marvelous light. We need to open ourselves to the searching, cleansing light of the Holy Spirit of God. The result is that while we used to live and walk in darkness and fear and misery, now we can live and walk in light and peace and joy. God will fill every part of our lives with His life-giving Spirit so that we can live free!

What a great feeling to get rid of the pretending.
No more putting on a facade and playing games.
It feels great to walk in the light!

FORGIVING
OTHERS

God has new plans on the horizon of your life, but you will never see them if you live with unforgiveness in your heart.

GOD'S WORD FOR YOU

But He gives us more and more grace (power of the Holy Spirit, to meet this evil tendency and all others fully). That is why He says, God sets Himself against the proud and haughty, but gives grace [continually] to the lowly (those who are humble enough to receive it).

JAMES 4:6

three

FORGIVING OTHERS

have read that medical studies indicate that 75 percent of physical sickness is caused by emotional problems. And one of the greatest emotional problems people experience is guilt. Many people are punishing themselves with sickness. They are refusing to relax and enjoy life because, after all, they don't *deserve* to have a good time. So they live in perpetual penance of regret and remorse. This kind of stress makes people sick.

There are two things that cause us to get all knotted up inside. The first is the negative things done to us by others. The second is the negative things we have done to ourselves and others. We have a hard time getting over what others have done to us, and we find it difficult to forget what we have done to ourselves and others.

Many years ago I had a choice to remain bitter, full of hatred and self-pity, resenting the people who had hurt and abused me as well as those who were able to enjoy nice, normal lives, those who had never been hurt as I was. Or, I could choose to follow God's path, allowing Him to make me a better person because of what I had been through. I thank Him that He gave me the grace to make it through and follow His way rather than Satan's way.

God's way is forgiveness.

GOD'S WORD FOR YOU

*Then he answered and spake unto me, saying,
This is the word of the LORD unto Zerubbabel, saying,
Not by might, nor by power, but by my spirit, saith the
LORD of hosts.*

ZECHARIAH 4:6 KJV

They who sow in tears shall reap in joy and singing.

PSALM 126:5

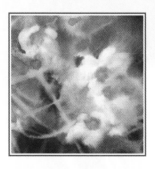

$\mathscr{D}$OORWAYS OF PAIN

For many of us, forgiving someone who has hurt us is the most difficult part of emotional healing. It can even be the stumbling block that prevents it. Those who have been badly wounded by others know that it is much easier to say the word *forgive* than it is to do it.

First, let me say that it is not possible to have good emotional health while harboring bitterness, resentment, and unforgiveness toward someone. It's poison to your system. And it is impossible to get better if it's there.

When I finally allowed the Lord to begin to work in my life, He revealed to me I had been hiding behind "doorways of pain"—the painful events and situations of my past. To pass back through the same, or similar, doorways and be delivered and healed meant facing the issues, people, and truths I found so difficult, if not impossible, to face on my own.

Don't be afraid of the pain. The temptation is to run away, but the Lord says that we are to go through our problems. Let your pain lead you out of bondage, not deeper into it. Endure whatever you need to, knowing that there is joy on the other side.

God does not bring hurts and wounds upon us.
But if they are inflicted upon us,
He is able to make miracles out of mistakes.

GOD'S WORD FOR YOU

Let all bitterness and indignation and wrath (passion, rage, bad temper) and resentment (anger, animosity) and quarreling (brawling, clamor, contention) and slander (evil-speaking, abusive or blasphemous language) be banished from you, with all malice (spite, ill will, or baseness of any kind).

And become useful and helpful and kind to one another, tenderhearted (compassionate, understanding, loving-hearted), forgiving one another [readily and freely], as God in Christ forgave you.

EPHESIANS 4:31–32

If you forgive anyone anything, I too forgive that one; and what I have forgiven, if I have forgiven anything, has been for your sakes in the presence [and with the approval] of Christ (the Messiah),

To keep Satan from getting the advantage over us; for we are not ignorant of his wiles and intentions.

2 CORINTHIANS 2:10–11

ℬE QUICK TO FORGIVE

The Bible teaches us to forgive "readily and freely." That is His standard for us, no matter how we feel about it. We are to be quick to forgive.

According to 1 Peter 5:5, we are to clothe ourselves with the character of Jesus Christ, meaning that we are to be long-suffering, patient, not easily offended, slow to anger, quick to forgive, and filled with mercy.

My definition of "mercy" is the ability to look beyond what is done to discover the reason why it was done. Many times people do things even they don't understand themselves, but there is always a reason why people behave as they do.

The same is true of us as believers. We are to be merciful and forgiving, just as God in Christ forgives us our wrongdoing—even when we don't understand why we do what we do.

The choice to forgive others is ours. He will not force anyone to do it. Even if you don't understand it, choose to follow it, believing that God's way is the best. It works. He can take what Satan meant to destroy you and turn it to your good. You must believe that or you will despair (Psalm 27:13).

We are to forgive in order to keep Satan from getting the advantage over us.

GOD'S WORD FOR YOU

Exercise foresight and be on the watch to look [after one another], to see that no one falls back from and fails to secure God's grace (His unmerited favor and spiritual blessing), in order that no root of resentment (rancor, bitterness, or hatred) shoots forth and causes trouble and bitter torment, and the many become contaminated and defiled by it . . .

HEBREWS 12:15

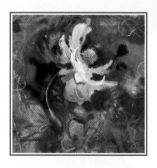

A ROOT OF BITTERNESS

When we allow unforgiveness in our lives, we are filled with resentment and bitterness. *Bitterness* refers to something that is pungent or sharp to the taste.

We remember that when the children of Israel were about to be led out of Egypt, they were told by the Lord on the eve of their departure to prepare a Passover meal that included bitter herbs. Why? God wanted them to eat those bitter herbs as a reminder of the bitterness they had experienced in bondage. Bitterness always goes hand in hand with bondage.

How does bitterness get started? It grows from a root, which *The King James Version* speaks of as a *root of bitterness*. A root of bitterness from the seed of unforgiveness always produces the fruit of bitterness.

Bitterness results from the many minor offenses we just can't let go of, the things we rehearse over and over inside us until they have become blown way out of proportion. And it comes from the major offenses people commit against us. The longer we allow them to grow and fester, the more powerful they become.

*A root of bitterness will infect our entire being —
our personality, our attitude and behavior,
our perspective, and our relationships,
especially our relationship with God.*

GOD'S WORD FOR YOU

And you shall hallow the fiftieth year and proclaim liberty throughout all the land to all its inhabitants. It shall be a jubilee for you . . .

And if your brother becomes poor beside you and sells himself to you, you shall not compel him to serve as a bondman (a slave not eligible for redemption).

But as a hired servant and as a temporary resident he shall be with you; he shall serve you till the Year of Jubilee,

And then he shall depart from you, he and his children with him, and shall go back to his own family and return to the possession of his fathers.

LEVITICUS 25:10, 39–41

And whenever you stand praying, if you have anything against anyone, forgive him and let it drop (leave it, let it go), in order that your Father Who is in heaven may also forgive you your [own] failings and shortcomings and let them drop.

MARK 11:25

*L*ET IT GO!

Do yourself a favor and let the offense and the offender go! To forgive is to keep yourself from being poisoned and imprisoned. To forgive is to excuse or pardon a fault or offense.

When a person is found guilty of a crime and sentenced to prison, we say he owes a debt to society. But if he is pardoned, he is allowed to go his way freely with no restraints upon him. Such a pardon cannot be earned, it must be granted by a higher authority.

When someone hurts us, we react as though that individual has stolen something from us. We feel they owe us. Yet Jesus told us we should let it go. We should drop it. And He taught us to pray in the Lord's Prayer, "Forgive us our debts, as we forgive our debtors."

In Leviticus 25 we read about the Year of Jubilee in which all debts were forgiven and all debtors were pardoned and set free in Israel. When we are in Christ, every day can be a Year of Jubilee if we are willing.

It is time to release that person from their debt and let it and them go. It is time to allow the Year of Jubilee to be celebrated in our lives.

The good news of the Cross is that Jesus paid the debt for us. God can say to us, "You don't owe Me anything anymore!"

GOD'S WORD FOR YOU

Then Jesus said to them again, Peace to you! [Just] as the Father has sent Me forth, so I am sending you.

And having said this, He breathed on them and said to them, Receive the Holy Spirit!

[Now having received the Holy Spirit, and being led and directed by Him] if you forgive the sins of anyone, they are forgiven; if you retain the sins of anyone, they are retained.

JOHN 20:21–23

ℛECEIVE THE HOLY SPIRIT'S HELP

The number one rule in forgiving sin is to receive the Holy Spirit, Who provides the strength and ability to forgive. None of us can do that on our own.

In John 20, I believe when Jesus breathed on the disciples and they received the Holy Spirit, they were born again at that moment. The next thing He said to them was that whatever sins they forgave were forgiven and whatever sins they retained were retained. The forgiving of sins seems to be the first power conferred upon people when they become born again. If that is so, then the forgiving of sins is our first duty as believers.

After realizing that you cannot forgive apart from the Holy Spirit's help, pray and release the person who hurt you. Repeat this prayer aloud: "Holy Spirit, breathe on me and give me strength. I forgive (name) for (whatever was done to you). I loose this person from their debt. I choose to walk in Your ways, Lord. I love You, and I turn this situation over to You. I cast my care upon You, and I believe You for my total restoration. Help me, Lord. Heal me of all the wounds inflicted upon me."

Now by faith leave it all in your Father's hands.

On our journey to wholeness, we are usually all knotted up inside. As we forgive, Jesus begins to straighten up our lives by untying one knot at a time.

GOD'S WORD FOR YOU

You have heard that it was said, You shall love your neighbor and hate your enemy;

But I tell you, Love your enemies and pray for those who persecute you . . .

MATTHEW 5:43–44

Invoke blessings upon and pray for the happiness of those who curse you, implore God's blessing (favor) upon those who abuse you [who revile, reproach, disparage, and high-handedly misuse you].

LUKE 6:28

Bless those who persecute you [who are cruel in their attitude toward you]; bless and do not curse them.

ROMANS 12:14

BLESS, NOT CURSE

Do you see what is missing when we just forgive someone and go no further? God in His Word instructs us to *forgive* others and then to *bless* them.

In this context, the word *bless* means "to speak well of." It is extending mercy to people who do not deserve it. And we are to pray for them to be blessed spiritually. We are to ask God to bring truth and revelation to them about their attitude and behavior so they will be willing to repent and be set free from their sins.

Revenge says, "You mistreated me, so I will mistreat you." Mercy says, "You mistreated me, so I'm going to forgive you, restore you, and treat you as if you never hurt me." What a blessing to be able to give and receive mercy. Give mercy and you will receive mercy.

Mercy is an attribute of God that is seen in how He deals with His people. Mercy is good to us when we deserve judgment. Mercy accepts and blesses us when we deserve to be totally rejected. Mercy understands our weaknesses and does not judge us.

The power of forgiveness will never work if we say we forgive but then turn around and curse the offender with our tongues or rehash the offense with others.

GOD'S WORD FOR YOU

Do not be unequally yoked with unbelievers [do not make mismated alliances with them or come under a different yoke with them, inconsistent with your faith]. For what partnership have right living and right standing with God with iniquity and lawlessness? Or how can light have fellowship with darkness?

What harmony can there be between Christ and Belial [the devil]? Or what has a believer in common with an unbeliever?

2 CORINTHIANS 6:14–15

FORGIVENESS AND RESTORATION

Many people have the mistaken idea that if someone has hurt them and they forgive that person, they will have to go back and suffer through the same hurt all over again. They think that in order to forgive, they must enter back into an active relationship with the person who has injured them. That is not true, and this misconception has caused a problem for many people who want to forgive.

Forgiveness does not necessarily mean restoration. If the relationship can be restored, and it is within God's will for it to be restored, then restoration is the best plan. But a broken relationship cannot always be restored. Sometimes it would not even be wise, especially in cases where abuse has been involved. It may even be dangerous.

In my own case, although I forgave my father who abused me and eventually tried to have fellowship with him, he made it clear he did not think he had ever done anything wrong. In fact, although he has now repented, at that time he went so far as to blame me for what happened. Without repentance on his part, that relationship could not have been reconciled.

Don't get caught in a trap that will open your wound and cause it to start bleeding again.

GOD'S WORD FOR YOU

Be still and rest in the Lord; wait for Him and patiently lean yourself upon Him; fret not yourself because of him who prospers in his way, because of the man who brings wicked devices to pass.

Cease from anger and forsake wrath; fret not yourself—it tends only to evildoing.

PSALM 37:7–8

It shall be said in that day, Behold our God upon Whom we have waited and hoped, that He might save us! This is the Lord, we have waited for Him; we will be glad and rejoice in His salvation.

ISAIAH 25:9

FORGIVENESS VERSUS FEELINGS

I believe that the greatest deception in the area of forgiveness Satan has perpetuated in the church is the idea that if a person's feelings have not changed, he has not forgiven. Many people believe this deception. They decide to forgive someone who has harmed them, but the devil convinces them that because they still have the same feelings toward the person, they have not fully forgiven that individual.

You can make all the correct decisions and for a long time not "feel" any different from the way you felt before you decided to forgive. This is where faith is needed to carry you through. You have done your part and now you are waiting for God to do His. His part is to heal your emotions, to make you feel well and not wounded. Only God has the power to change your feelings toward the person who hurt you.

Waiting is where the battle is won in the spiritual realm. Waiting and keeping your eyes on God will put pressure on the demonic forces that initiated the problem to begin with, and they have to give back the ground they had gained. Healing takes time!

You can make a decision to obey God, but you can't change how you feel. God will do that over time.

RESTORING THE SOUL

*For change to be lasting, it must come
from the inside out. Only God can cause
that type of heart change. Let God be God.*

GOD'S WORD FOR YOU

The Lord is my Shepherd [to feed, guide, and shield me], I shall not lack.

He makes me lie down in [fresh, tender] green pastures; He leads me beside the still and restful waters.

He refreshes and restores my life (my self); He leads me in the paths of righteousness [uprightness and right standing with Him—not for my earning it, but] for His name's sake.

PSALM 23:1–3

four
RESTORING THE SOUL

he Twenty-third Psalm is so comforting. In it the psalmist David tells us it is the Lord Who leads us, Who feeds, guides, and shields us. Who causes us to lie down and rest, Who refreshes and restores our soul.

It is through the power of forgiveness that God leads us in the paths of righteousness, uprightness, and right standing with Him. David is saying that God leads each of us in the path right for us individually. If we will allow Him to do so, He will guide us by His Holy Spirit into the unique path that leads to the fulfillment of His planned destiny for us.

Through the doorway of forgiveness, God refreshes and restores our soul or our life. It is with our soul that our body contacts the world, primarily through our personality, and it is with our spirit that we contact God. *Webster's Dictionary* tells us that the word *restore* means: "1. To bring back into existence or use. 2. To bring back to an original state. 3. To put back in a former position. 4. To make restitution of: give back."

God promises restoration of what was lost or ruined through unforgiveness. I can verify He keeps His promises.

You have a blood-bought right to enjoy your life. Be determined to keep the power of forgiveness working its freedom in your life.

GOD'S WORD FOR YOU

For we are God's [own] handiwork (His workmanship), recreated in Christ Jesus, [born anew] that we may do those good works which God predestined (planned beforehand) for us [taking paths which He prepared ahead of time], that we should walk in them [living the good life which He prearranged and made ready for us to live].

EPHESIANS 2:10

For I know the thoughts and plans that I have for you, says the Lord, thoughts and plans for welfare and peace and not for evil, to give you hope in your final outcome.

JEREMIAH 29:11

God's Predestined Plan

God had a good plan laid out for each of us before we made our appearance on this planet. God's unique plan for each of us is not a plan of failure, misery, poverty, sickness, and disease. His plan is a good plan, a plan for life and health, happiness, and fulfillment.

In John 10:10 Jesus said, "The thief comes only in order to steal and kill and destroy. I came that they may have and enjoy life, and have it in abundance." The devil comes to disrupt that plan and to destroy the good thing God has in mind for us.

God's good plan may have been disrupted in our lives, but we need to understand His heart and the restorative power of His forgiveness. He doesn't like it when someone hurts us and tries to undermine His plan for us. It should be a great comfort to us to know that while He is making us lie down in green pastures to restore our soul, He is working on our behalf concerning our situation!

If we will trust the Lord, He will do for us what we cannot do for ourselves. Only He has the power to restore what has been lost to us, whether that loss was our fault or the fault of our enemy.

GOD'S WORD FOR YOU

But the Comforter (Counselor, Helper, Intercessor, Advocate, Strengthener, Standby), the Holy Spirit, Whom the Father will send in My name [in My place, to represent Me and act on My behalf], He will teach you all things. And He will cause you to recall (will remind you of, bring to your remembrance) everything I have told you.

JOHN 14:26

$\mathscr{M}$EMORIES

The basic meaning of the word *restore* is "to turn back (hence, away) . . . literally or figuratively (not necessarily with the idea of return to the starting point)." God wants to take us back to the point of departure, the place where we veered from His plan for us, then bring us forward to make things work out the way He intended from the beginning. He will not necessarily take us back to the place physically, and often does not. I don't think He even wants us to try to go there in our memory and relive that experience, although perhaps some people need to do that if there is a memory that has been blocked and needs to be faced.

There are things about my childhood I cannot recall, and it doesn't bother me a bit. Some things are better off not being remembered or relived. Many times a God-given ability to forget is a real blessing.

One facet of the ministry of the Holy Spirit is to bring things to our remembrance. Rather than digging into our past, we must trust God to bring only the right things to our attention.

It is dangerous to go back into your subconscious and dig up all kinds of harmful and hurtful memories. Trust the Holy Spirit to bring forth only those things that need to be dealt with.

GOD'S WORD FOR YOU

When Joseph had come to his brothers, they stripped him of his [distinctive] long garment which he was wearing;

Then they took him and cast him into the [well-like] pit which was empty; there was no water in it.

GENESIS 37:23–24

And Pharaoh said to Joseph, Forasmuch as [your] God has shown you all this, there is nobody as intelligent and discreet and understanding and wise as you are.

You shall have charge over my house, and all my people shall be governed according to your word [with reverence, submission, and obedience]. Only in matters of the throne will I be greater than you are.

GENESIS 41:39–40

FROM THE PIT TO THE PALACE

A pit is a ditch, a trap, or a snare. It refers to destruction. Satan always wants to bring us into the pit.

Joseph was sold into slavery by his brothers who hated him. They actually threw him into a pit and intended to leave him there to die, but God had other plans. He ended up being sold into slavery in Egypt, where he was abused and ended up in prison for refusing to compromise his integrity. Yet everywhere Joseph went, God gave him favor. Ultimately, he ended up in the palace, second in command to Pharaoh.

How did Joseph get from the pit to the palace? I believe it was by remaining positive, refusing to be bitter, and being confident and trusting God. Even though it looked like he was defeated on many occasions, he kept standing up on the inside.

Joseph had a right attitude. Without a right attitude, a person can start in the palace and end up in a pit, which actually happens to a lot of people. Some, it seems, have great opportunities given to them, and they do nothing with their lives, while others who get a very bad start in life overcome all obstacles and succeed.

No matter where you started, you can have a great finish! I challenge you to do something great for God.

GOD'S WORD FOR YOU

As for you, you thought evil against me, but God meant it for good, to bring about that many people should be kept alive, as they are this day.

GENESIS 50:20

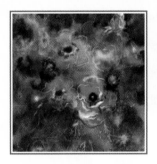

Good from Bad

God wants to restore your soul. One way or another, He wants to go back to where your life got off track and make everything right from that moment forward.

Joseph is the classic biblical example of how God takes what was meant for evil against us and works it out for our good. In that dramatic scene where Joseph is speaking in Genesis 50:20, he tells his brothers that what they meant to him as evil, and was truly evil, God had used for good to save them and their families and hundreds of thousands of others in a time of famine.

In my own life, I cannot truthfully say I am glad I was abused. But through the power of forgiveness and yielding my abuse to God, He has healed me and made me a better, stronger, more spiritually powerful and sensitive person. He has restored my soul and driven out the fear and insecurity. I can trust, love, forgive, and live with simplicity in my approach to life. I am free to enjoy what I do.

Only God can bring good from bad.

Although even the Lord cannot change what has happened to you, He can change the consequences of it.

GOD'S WORD FOR YOU

The Spirit of the Lord God is upon me, because the Lord has anointed and qualified me to preach the Gospel of good tidings to the meek, the poor, and afflicted; He has sent me to bind up and heal the brokenhearted, to proclaim liberty to the [physical and spiritual] captives and the opening of the prison and of the eyes to those who are bound,

To proclaim the acceptable year of the Lord [the year of His favor] and the day of vengeance of our God, to comfort all who mourn,

To grant [consolation and joy] to those who mourn in Zion—to give them an ornament (a garland or diadem) of beauty instead of ashes, the oil of joy instead of mourning, the garment [expressive] of praise instead of a heavy, burdened, and failing spirit—that they may be called oaks of righteousness [lofty, strong, and magnificent, distinguished for uprightness, justice, and right standing with God], the planting of the Lord, that He may be glorified.

ISAIAH 61:1–3

78

OPENING THE ASHES

Here in Isaiah 61:3 we are told that as part of His restoration process, the Lord gives beauty for ashes. But for that to happen to us, we must be willing to give Him the ashes.

You may have been hurt in the past and have kept the ashes of that hurt somewhere close at hand. Every once in a while you may get them out and re-grieve over them. If so, I understand because I used to do the same thing.

But you need to do what I did and let go of these ashes, allowing the wind of the Holy Spirit to blow them away to where they cannot be found again. This is a new day. There is no more time left for grieving over the ashes of the past. You have no future dwelling in your past.

God has the same good plan for you that He had the moment you arrived on this planet. He has never changed His mind, and He never will. From the very moment the enemy hurt you, God has had your restoration in His heart. Know that you are valuable, unique, loved, and special in His eyes!

Allow the Holy Spirit to blow away the ashes that are left behind from Satan's attempt to destroy you and replace those ashes with beauty.

GOD'S WORD FOR YOU

Yes, though I walk through the [deep, sunless] valley of the shadow of death, I will fear or dread no evil, for You are with me; Your rod [to protect] and Your staff [to guide], they comfort me.

You prepare a table before me in the presence of my enemies. You anoint my head with oil; my [brimming] cup runs over.

Surely or only goodness, mercy, and unfailing love shall follow me all the days of my life, and through the length of my days the house of the Lord [and His presence] shall be my dwelling place.

PSALM 23:4–6

My Cup Runneth Over!

I love the words in the last part of David's most beloved hymn of praise to God in Psalm 23. He describes the condition the Lord wants us to be in constantly. He wants us to be protected, guided, and comforted. He wants to set a table of blessings before us in the very face of our enemies. He wants to anoint us with the oil of joy instead of mourning. He wants our cup of blessings to overflow continually in thanksgiving and praise to Him for His goodness, mercy, and unfailing love toward us. And He wants us to live forever, moment by moment, in His Holy presence.

All these "wants" are a part of His good plan for each of us. Regardless of how far we may have fallen, He wants to raise us up and restore us to that right and perfect plan He has for our lives.

It would benefit every one of us if we would say to ourselves several times a day, "God has a fantastic plan for my life. I want all that He wants for me. I receive His anointing of the Holy Spirit to fill my cup and overflow. I will walk and live in the presence of the Lord."

Remember that the most important thing
in receiving God's blessings is not our great faith
but His great faithfulness.

GOD'S WORD FOR YOU

You shall not need to fight in this battle; take your positions, stand still, and see the deliverance of the Lord [Who is] with you. . . . Fear not nor be dismayed. Tomorrow go out against them, for the Lord is with you.

And Jehoshaphat bowed his head with his face to the ground, and all Judah and the inhabitants of Jerusalem fell down before the Lord, worshiping Him.

And some Levites . . . stood up to praise the Lord, the God of Israel, with a very loud voice.

And they rose early in the morning and went out into the Wilderness of Tekoa; and as they went out, Jehoshaphat stood and said, Hear me, O Judah . . . Believe in the Lord your God and you shall be established; believe and remain steadfast to His prophets and you shall prosper.

When he had consulted with the people, he appointed singers to sing to the Lord and praise Him in their holy [priestly] garments as they went out before the army, saying, Give thanks to the Lord, for His mercy and loving-kindness endure forever!

2 CHRONICLES 20:17–21

RESTORED TO WORSHIP

Through the power of forgiveness we enter into God's rest and take our position in Jesus Christ. We find that He is our peace, our justification, and our provider. It is the joy of the Lord that is our strength. He does not just give us joy; He is our joy and our hope. We are to abide in Jesus and bless and worship Him.

Worship transforms us. By starting to worship God for the changes that He is already working in us, we find that those changes start manifesting more and more, and we experience new levels of God's glory, which is the manifestation of all His excellencies. In other words, God will pour His goodness out upon the worshiper.

There is a release that comes through worship. Sometimes we need a mental or emotional release. As we worship the Lord, we release our emotional or mental burden that is weighing us down. It is swallowed up in the awesomeness of God.

Begin to worship early in the morning. Worship while you are getting ready for work, and when you are on your way to work. You will be amazed to see how things begin to change at home and on the job.

Worship creates an atmosphere where God can work.

GOD'S WORD FOR YOU

I thank God Whom I worship with a pure conscience, in the spirit of my fathers, when without ceasing I remember you night and day in my prayers . . .

2 TIMOTHY 1:3

Therefore I always exercise and discipline myself [mortifying my body, deadening my carnal affections, bodily appetites, and worldly desires, endeavoring in all respects] to have a clear (unshaken, blameless) conscience, void of offense toward God and toward men.

ACTS 24:16

A RESTORED CONSCIENCE

The restoration of true worship must come from the heart of the worshiper. It is not, and can never be, merely a learned behavior. God is interested in the heart of man above all else. If the heart is not pure, nothing that comes from the man is acceptable to God.

Paul spoke of the importance of keeping one's conscience clean. We cannot properly worship God with known sin in our lives. We must approach God with a clean conscience.

There is no peace for the person with a guilty conscience. His faith will not work; therefore, his prayers won't be answered. His excuses for sin will never stand in the presence of God.

One of the main functions of the Holy Spirit is to teach us all truth, to convict us of sin, and to convince us of righteousness (John 16:8, 13). Conviction is not meant to condemn; it is rather intended to provoke us to repentance. Through repentance and the power of forgiveness, our conscience is cleansed and purified. What good news! We can live before God with a perfectly clear conscience.

Let your conscience be your friend,
not a source of torment. Ask God to give you
a tender conscience toward Him.

DEALING
WITH SHAME

❧

You cannot get beyond your own opinion of yourself—no matter how many good things God may say about you in His Word. Regardless of all the wonderful plans He may have for your life, none of them will come to pass without your cooperation.

GOD'S WORD FOR YOU

Therefore if any person is [ingrafted] in Christ (the Messiah) he is a new creation (a new creature altogether); the old [previous moral and spiritual condition] has passed away. Behold, the fresh and new has come! . . .

For our sake He made Christ [virtually] to be sin Who knew no sin, so that in and through Him we might become [endued with, viewed as being in, and examples of] the righteousness of God [what we ought to be, approved and acceptable and in right relationship with Him, by His goodness].

2 CORINTHIANS 5:17, 21

five
DEALING WITH SHAME

n my personal life, one area that I found to be very difficult to deal with was that of guilt and shame. I have previously addressed it in part, but I must expand upon it. In my many dealings with people, I have found the confusion surrounding this issue to be a huge problem to those who should be enjoying the power of forgiveness in their lives.

I carried a sense of guilt as long I could remember. Guilt was my constant companion. We went everywhere together! It began early in my childhood when I was being sexually abused. Even though my abuser told me that what he was doing was not wrong, it made me feel dirty and guilty. That only increased as I got older and became aware of just how wrong it was. I can never remember being guilt-free, even if I wasn't doing anything bad.

If you were told over and over as a youth that you were no good, there was something wrong with you, you couldn't do anything right, you were worthless and would never amount to anything, it is very possible you began to believe it and those thoughts took root in your life.

If your life was rooted in shame,
the power of forgiveness extends
to the deepest root.

GOD'S WORD FOR YOU

My dishonor is before me all day long, and shame has covered my face . . .

PSALM 44:15

ROOTED SHAME

There is a shame that is normal and healthy. If I lose or break something that belongs to someone else, I feel ashamed of my mistake. I am sorry, but I can ask forgiveness, receive it, and then go on with my life. Healthy shame reminds us that we are human beings with weaknesses and limitations.

In the Garden of Eden after the fall, Adam and Eve were ashamed when they realized they were naked (Genesis 3:6–8). They went and hid and tried to cover themselves. But that too was a normal reaction. If we sin, we feel bad about it until we repent and are forgiven.

But when an individual is rooted in shame, it poisons his entire life. He is not just ashamed of what he has done, he is ashamed of who he is. This person takes the shame into himself where it actually becomes the core of his being. Everything in his life becomes poisoned by his emotions so that he develops into a shame-based person.

The power of grace and forgiveness was sent to free us from the shame that would have us believe that something is wrong with us.

GOD'S WORD FOR YOU

*For each tree is known and identified by its own fruit;
for figs are not gathered from thornbushes, nor is a cluster
of grapes picked from a bramblebush.*

*The upright (honorable, intrinsically good) man out
of the good treasure [stored] in his heart produces what is
upright (honorable and intrinsically good), and the evil
man out of the evil storehouse brings forth that which is
depraved (wicked and intrinsically evil); for out of the
abundance (overflow) of the heart his mouth speaks.*

LUKE 6:44–45

FRUIT OF SHAME

For the person who is rooted in shame, sooner or later the fruit will begin to manifest itself. Often in our fear of being seen for who we think we are, we try to be one way for one person or group and a totally different way for another. In our process of trying to avoid rejection by pleasing others, we lose track of who we really are and end up confused and miserable.

If we believe and feel that who we are is not acceptable, we may begin to hide our true feelings. Some people become so adept at repressing their true feelings they become emotionally frozen, unable to express any kind of feeling or emotion at all because it is too painful to do so. How many men put on a "macho" front and will not show any tenderness or sensitivity for fear they might appear weak or wimpish?

I found that I always felt defeated because no matter what I accomplished on the outside, I still felt bad about myself on the inside. I was ashamed of me! I didn't like who I was. I was continually rejecting my real self and trying to be someone or something I was not and never could be. That's the bad fruit of shame.

It's time to come out from behind our masks and become real. Only the Holy Spirit can teach us who we really are.

GOD'S WORD FOR YOU

May Christ through your faith [actually] dwell (settle down, abide, make His permanent home) in your hearts! May you be rooted deep in love and founded securely on love.

EPHESIANS 3:17

OUR "LOVE TANK"

Each one of us is born with a "love tank," and if our tank is empty, we are in trouble. We need to start receiving love from the moment we are born and continue receiving it—and giving it out—until the day we die.

Sometimes Satan manages to arrange things so that instead of receiving love, we receive hurts and abuse. If that arrangement continues, we become love-starved and warped, so that we are unable to maintain healthy relationships. If we can't get good feelings from within ourselves, we look for them on the outside. Many develop addictive behaviors of different types to try to find that inner satisfaction. They turn to sex, drugs, alcohol, tobacco, food, money, power, work, television, sports, and other addictive things to try to get some good feelings about themselves.

The good news is that whatever we may have been deprived of in the past, we can receive from the Lord. He is our Shepherd, so we shall not want (Psalm 23:1). He has promised not to withhold any good thing from us (Psalm 84:11). We can become rooted in His love and not rooted and grounded in the bad fruit tree of shame.

We don't have to go through another moment of our life with an empty "love tank." Receiving the love of God is the key.

GOD'S WORD FOR YOU

Blessed (happy, blithesome, joyous, spiritually prosperous—with life-joy and satisfaction in God's favor and salvation, regardless of their outward conditions) are the meek (the mild, patient, long-suffering), for they shall inherit the earth!

MATTHEW 5:5

TRUE MEEKNESS

A root of shame always manifests itself in abnormal ways. Bitterness, anger, and hostility produce pent-up emotions that don't get released properly. Some people actually think they deserve being taken advantage of and become doormats for everybody. They are mousy and wimpish.

I was not like that. I didn't even know who to be mad at. All I knew was that I was angry, and I was hurt. I was tired of being mistreated, and I wasn't going to take anything from anybody. I was always near what I call the "explode point." All it took was for someone to cross or offend me, or for something to go wrong, and I was ready to "blow up."

God wants to root our lives in the meekness of Jesus. We see in His life the power to repress and express anger at the right times. Meekness is the middle ground between emotional extremes. Meekness never allows anger to get out of control. It channels it in the right direction for the right purpose. We need to direct our anger away from people and ourselves and focus it on the source of our problem, the devil and his demons (Ephesians 6:12).

True meekness is getting angry at the right time in the right measure for the right reason.

GOD'S WORD FOR YOU

According as he hath chosen us in him before the foundation of the world, that we should be holy and without blame before him in love: . . .

To the praise of the glory of his grace, wherein he hath made us accepted in the beloved.

EPHESIANS 1:4, 6 KJV

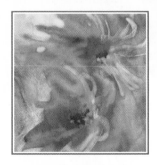

ACCEPTED IN THE BELOVED

I remember standing in a prayer line where I overheard a woman next to me telling a pastor how she hated and despised herself. The pastor shocked her and me by stopping her and saying, "Who do you think you are? You have no right to hate yourself. God loved you so much that He sent His only Son to die for you . . . to suffer in your place. You have no right to hate or reject yourself. Your part is to receive what Jesus died to give you!"

Sometimes it takes a strong word to get us to see a trap that Satan has set for us. Self-rejection and self-hatred can almost sound pious to the shame-based person. They can become a way of punishing ourselves for our failures and inabilities.

God ordained us, destined us, planned in love for us to be adopted and accepted as His own children through His Son, Jesus Christ! Before we even existed, He chose us and set us apart to be blameless in His sight, above reproach before Him in love. With that knowledge, we should have our "love tanks" filled to overflowing!

Jesus bore your sins and shame and hatred and condemnation on the cross. What a glorious truth!

GOD'S WORD FOR YOU

For God so greatly loved and dearly prized the world that He [even] gave up His only begotten (unique) Son, so that whoever believes in (trusts in, clings to, relies on) Him shall not perish (come to destruction, be lost) but have eternal (everlasting) life.

JOHN 3:16

You shall love your neighbor as [you do] yourself.

MATTHEW 19:19

ℒOVING YOURSELF

I believe one of the greatest problems people have today concerns the way they feel about themselves. The truth is that most people carry around with them bad attitudes and negative self-images. Many of them have carried the negatives so long they don't even realize they have them.

What do you think of yourself? What kind of relationship do you have with yourself? No matter where you go or what you do in this life, you are always going to have to deal with you. There is no escaping from you.

The Lord commanded us to love ourselves as we love our neighbors. Many of us think we have worn God out with our failures and messes, but you can't do that. He loves us because He is Love. We need to love and accept ourselves as His creation. It begins when we are transplanted into His love and are rooted in Jesus. May He be your foundation and your root, so you will produce good fruit.

Receive God's love for you.
Bathe in it. Meditate on it.
Let it change and strengthen you.
Then give it away.

GOD'S WORD FOR YOU

Fear not, for you shall not be ashamed; neither be confounded and depressed, for you shall not be put to shame. For you shall forget the shame of your youth, and you shall not [seriously] remember the reproach of your widowhood any more.

ISAIAH 54:4

$\mathscr{L}$IKING YOURSELF

It is not enough to love ourselves; we must also like ourselves. If you don't like yourself, you are going to have a hard time liking anyone else. If you're unhappy with yourself, you'll have trouble with others. You may pretend things are fine, but pretense doesn't alter the fact.

Because we are rooted and grounded in love, we can be relaxed and at ease, knowing that our acceptance is not based on our performance or perfect behavior. We can be secure in the knowledge that our value and worth are not dependent upon who we are or what we think or say or do. It is based on our relationship with Jesus.

To like ourselves simply means we accept ourselves as God's creation. We accept the fact that though we fail, that doesn't mean we are any less God's child.

Look at yourself in the mirror every morning and say, "I like you. You are a child of God. He loves you for who you are. You have gifts and talents. You are a neat person—and I like you." If you do that and really believe it, it will work wonders in overcoming a shame-based nature.

We need to be at peace with our past,
content with our present, and sure about our future,
knowing they are in God's loving hands.

GOD'S WORD FOR YOU

Instead of your [former] shame you shall have a twofold recompense; instead of dishonor and reproach [your people] shall rejoice in their portion. Therefore in their land they shall possess double [what they had forfeited]; everlasting joy shall be theirs.

ISAIAH 61:7

A TWOFOLD RECOMPENSE

If you are convinced that you have a shame-based nature or that you are rooted and grounded in shame, that curse can be broken off of you through the power of God. In Isaiah 54:4 and Isaiah 61:7, the Lord has promised to remove the shame and dishonor from us so that we remember it no more. He has promised that in their place He will pour out upon us a twofold blessing so that we possess double what we have lost, and that everlasting joy shall be ours.

Take your stand on the Word of God. Ask the Lord to work a healing miracle in your mind, will, and emotions. Let Him come in and fulfill what He came to do: heal your broken heart, bind up your wounds, give you beauty for ashes, joy for mourning, a garment of praise instead of heaviness, a double honor for a double shame.

Determine that from this moment on you are going to reject the roots of bitterness, shame, negativism, and perfectionism, and be rooted and grounded in the love of Christ.

Draw the bloodline of Jesus Christ across your life and boldly declare you are healed from the pains and wounds of your past and set free to live a new life of health and wholeness.

LIVING
FREE

*Refuse to live the rest of your life
in a prison of suspicion and fear! And
don't look to others to meet your needs.
Look to God. Anything people may do
to you, God can fix.*

GOD'S WORD FOR YOU

But Jesus [for His part] did not trust Himself to them, because He knew all [men];

And He did not need anyone to bear witness concerning man [needed no evidence from anyone about men], for He Himself knew what was in human nature. [He could read men's hearts.]

JOHN 2:24–25

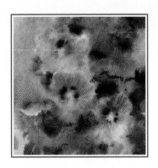

six

LIVING FREE

he power of forgiveness is the power of God to transform us from the inside out. Jesus is our example and role model for every aspect of our lives, and He demonstrated how we should live in relationship with other people.

Jesus did not trust people, because He knew human nature. He ate, drank, laughed, and wept with people. He confided in them and shared intimate things out of His heart with them. They were His friends, and He cared about them. But He did not trust Himself to them.

I think that means He did not become dependent upon them. He didn't throw Himself wide open to them. He didn't allow Himself to reach the place of feeling He could not get along without them. He purposely kept Himself in a position where He was primarily dependent upon God and God alone.

What the Lord is telling us is that He wants us to live our lives in balance. We must love our fellowman and maintain good fellowship with him. But we must never make the mistake of thinking we can trust others completely.

I cannot tell you, "Just trust people; they won't hurt you." We must face the reality that people hurt people.

GOD'S WORD FOR YOU

But far be it from me to glory [in anything or anyone] except in the cross of our Lord Jesus Christ (the Messiah), through Whom the world has been crucified to me, and I to the world!

GALATIANS 6:14

Thus says the Lord: Cursed [with great evil] is the strong man who trusts in and relies on frail man, making weak [human] flesh his arm, and whose mind and heart turn aside from the Lord.

JEREMIAH 17:5

KEEPING A PROPER BALANCE

The apostle Paul makes it clear he did not glory in anything or anyone, because the world was crucified to him and he to the world. What I think he meant was that he kept all things—including people, places, and positions—in proper balance in his life. He was not dependent upon anyone or anything for his joy and peace and victory in the Lord. He would not put pressure on relationships in an effort to get from people what only God could give him.

If we are not careful to maintain a proper balance in our lives, we will develop dependencies that Satan can play upon to destroy us and our effectiveness for Christ.

This is the balance God requires of us: When I look to myself to meet my needs, I fail; and when I look to others to meet my needs, they fail me. The Lord requires that He be allowed to meet our needs. When we look to Him, He often uses people to meet our needs, but we are looking to and depending on Him—not the people through whom He works.

Don't put pressure on other people
by expecting them to never disappoint,
fail, or hurt you.

GOD'S WORD FOR YOU

*And set your minds and keep them set on what is above
(the higher things), not on the things that are on the earth.*

*For [as far as this world is concerned] you have died,
and your [new, real] life is hidden with Christ in God.*

COLOSSIANS 3:2–3

ALIVE IN CHRIST

If you and I allow ourselves to become dependent on or addicted to things and people, the devil will use them to cause us all kinds of grief. That's why we must keep our eyes on Jesus and not on the things of this earth. As Paul was, you and I are "dead to this world" — and it is dead to us. We must not look to it for our help, but to the Lord.

You and I are never going to be whole and well mentally or emotionally or spiritually as long as we think we have to have some person or some thing. It might be nice to have them, but we don't have to have anybody or anything but God to get by!

Are you looking to people or things to make you happy? In my daily prayer sometimes I say, "Father, there is something I want, but I don't want to get out of balance or ahead of You. If it is Your will, I would like to have it. But if it is not Your will, then I can be happy without it because I want You to be number one in my life."

Trust God with the people in your life.
You may not be able to handle them,
but He is able.

GOD'S WORD FOR YOU

But be doers of the Word [obey the message], and not merely listeners to it, betraying yourselves [into deception by reasoning contrary to the Truth].

For if anyone only listens to the Word without obeying it and being a doer of it, he is like a man who looks carefully at his [own] natural face in a mirror;

For he thoughtfully observes himself, and then goes off and promptly forgets what he was like.

But he who looks carefully into the faultless law, the [law] of liberty, and is faithful to it and perseveres in looking into it, being not a heedless listener who forgets but an active doer [who obeys], he shall be blessed in his doing (his life of obedience).

JAMES 1:22–25

DOERS OF THE WORD

If you and I are to walk in the power and freedom of our forgiveness, we must become doers of the Word and not hearers only. Otherwise we are deceiving ourselves by going contrary to the truth.

It is the truth and the truth alone that will keep us set free. In order for that truth to work in our lives, we must be responsible. To receive what God promises us in His Word, we must obey the Word. We cannot try to excuse away our sins and weaknesses. Instead, we must become bond servants to God and not our human nature or to other people or things.

The bottom line is this: God is your Helper. He is your Healer. He has a personalized plan for your life in His Word. Make sure you know what it is, then begin to walk in obedience to the truth one step at a time. Obeying the Word requires consistency and diligence. It can't be hit and miss. We can't just try it to see if it works. There must be a dedication and commitment to do the Word whatever the outcome.

We will walk in victory if we do what the Lord says.

GOD'S WORD FOR YOU

Whoever will humble himself therefore and become like this little child [trusting, lowly, loving, forgiving] is greatest in the kingdom of heaven.

And whoever receives and accepts and welcomes one little child like this for My sake and in My name receives and accepts and welcomes Me.

MATTHEW 18:4–5

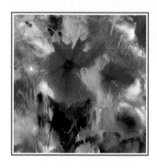

ℬECOME CHILDLIKE

You and I must humble ourselves and become as little children. While the Lord wants us to grow up in our attitude, behavior, and acceptance of responsibility in Christ (Ephesians 4:15), at the same time He wants us to be childlike in our dependence upon Him and in our free expression of our feelings toward Him.

One characteristic of a child is that he has fun no matter what he does. He manages to find a way to have a good time. God wants us to learn how to enjoy things and to enjoy Him. He wants us to enjoy prayer, Bible study, and going to church, just as He wants us to enjoy our spouse, children, family, home, and everything else in life, including the mundane. For too long we have put off enjoying life.

We need to find more humor in our everyday lives. And one of the first things we need to learn to laugh at is ourselves. Instead of getting all upset at our mistakes and shortcomings, we need to learn to laugh at our failures and foibles. As Art Linkletter used to say, "People are funny!" And that includes us.

Jesus wants us to walk in the freedom of little children.

GOD'S WORD FOR YOU

Now on the final and most important day of the Feast, Jesus stood, and He cried in a loud voice, If any man is thirsty, let him come to Me and drink!

He who believes in Me [who cleaves to and trusts in and relies on Me] as the Scripture has said, From his innermost being shall flow [continuously] springs and rivers of living water.

But He was speaking here of the Spirit, Whom those who believed (trusted, had faith) in Him were afterward to receive. For the [Holy] Spirit had not yet been given, because Jesus was not yet glorified (raised to honor).

JOHN 7:37–39

THE LIVING WATER

You and I are born with a nice, clean flowing well within us. Over time, Satan comes along and starts throwing stones into that well. By the time we are adults, our wells are so filled with stones that they have become stopped up. Every now and then we may feel a little gurgle down inside, but we never experience the water flowing freely.

Notice in John 7 that Jesus did not say that from those who believe in Him there will flow rivers of living water once in a while. He said these rivers of living water will flow continuously. That living water is the Holy Spirit. He quenches the deepest thirst of the soul.

That river of living water flows within all who have accepted Jesus as Lord and Savior. The Holy Spirit, that living water, empowers us to live according to God's will—a path that takes us to freedom.

Allowing the Holy Spirit to flow through you will not only water you but also those around you.

GOD'S WORD FOR YOU

Though the fig tree does not blossom and there is no fruit on the vines, [though] the product of the olive fails and the fields yield no food, though the flock is cut off from the fold and there are no cattle in the stalls,

Yet I will rejoice in the Lord; I will exult in the [victorious] God of my salvation!

The Lord God is my Strength, my personal bravery, and my invincible army; He makes my feet like hinds' feet and will make me to walk [not to stand still in terror, but to walk] and make [spiritual] progress upon my high places [of trouble, suffering, or responsibility]!

HABAKKUK 3:17–19

ℋang Tough!

The Old Testament prophet Habakkuk spoke of hard times, calling them "high places," and stating that God had given him hinds' feet to scale those high places. A "hind" refers to a certain kind of deer that is an agile mountain climber. It can scale up what looks like a sheer cliff, leaping from ledge to ledge with great ease.

This is God's will for us, that when hardship comes our way we are not intimidated or frightened. To be truly victorious, we must grow to the place where we are not afraid of hard times but are actually challenged by them. In these verses these "high places" are referred to as "trouble, suffering, or responsibility." This is because it is during these times that we grow.

If you look back over your life, you will see that you never grow during easy times; you grow during hard times. During the easy times that come, you are able to enjoy what you have gained during the hard times. This is really a life principle; it is just the way it works.

God desires to restore you and me
to our rightful position of authority.
We were born destined for the throne,
not the ash heap of life.

GOD'S WORD FOR YOU

When you pass through the waters, I will be with you, and through the rivers, they will not overwhelm you. When you walk through the fire, you will not be burned or scorched, nor will the flame kindle upon you.

ISAIAH 43:2

Go All the Way Through

God wants us to be diligent and go all the way through with Him, not just go until the way becomes difficult, and then stop there. One of our greatest challenges is to face our mountains rather than trying to go around them.

Sometimes we go around and around the same mountain, and we end up like the Israelites in the wilderness who wandered around for forty years (Deuteronomy 2:1–3). We must learn to face our mountains and determine to go all the way through with God. That is the only path to victory.

I encourage you to go all the way through with God no matter how difficult it may seem. Let God have His way in your life. Pray for God's will and not your own will. God's way is for you to set your face like a flint, dig in both heels, and go all the way through.

Determine to enjoy the journey. Enjoying life is an attitude of the heart, a decision to enjoy everything because everything—even little, seemingly insignificant things—has a part in God's plan for our lives.

As we believe that it is God's will for us to experience continual joy, we will discover a power that lifts us above life's circumstances.

GOD'S WORD FOR YOU

And, [His completed experience] making Him perfectly [equipped], He became the Author and Source of eternal salvation to all those who give heed and obey Him . . .

HEBREWS 5:9

Looking away [from all that will distract] to Jesus, Who is the Leader and the Source of our faith [giving the first incentive for our belief] and is also its Finisher [bringing it to maturity and perfection]. He, for the joy [of obtaining the prize] that was set before Him, endured the cross, despising and ignoring the shame, and is now seated at the right hand of the throne of God.

HEBREWS 12:2

124

BRIDGES INSTEAD OF WALLS

Instead of the walls that I used to build around my life, I have learned to build bridges. By the power of grace and God's forgiveness, all the difficult and unfair things that have happened to me have been turned into highways over which others can pass to find the same liberty that I found.

God is no respecter of persons (Acts 10:34). What He has done for me, He will do for you, as long as His precepts are followed. You can discover the same freedom that I have found, and you can become a bridge for others to pass over, instead of a wall that shuts them out.

Jesus pioneered a pathway to God for us. He became a highway for us to pass over. He sacrificed Himself for us, and now that we are benefiting from His sacrifice, He is giving us a chance to sacrifice for others so they can reap the same benefits we enjoy. When my way gets hard, I remind myself that Jesus endured the cross for the joy of obtaining the prize that was set before Him.

Make a decision to tear down your walls and build bridges. There are many people who are lost in their messes and need someone to go before them and show them the way. Why not be that person for them?

JOYCE MEYER

Joyce Meyer has been teaching the Word of God
since 1976 and in full-time ministry since 1980. She
is the bestselling author of over 54 inspirational
books, including *Secrets to Exceptional Living*, *The Joy
of Believing Prayer*, and *Battlefield of the Mind*, as well
as over 240 audiocassette albums and over 90 videos.
Joyce's *Life In The Word* radio and television
programs are broadcast around the world, and she
travels extensively conducting "Life In The Word"
conferences. Joyce and her husband, Dave, are
the parents of four grown children and make
their home in St. Louis, Missouri.

Additional copies of this book are available from your local bookstore.

If this book has changed your life, we would like to hear from you.

Please write us at:

Joyce Meyer Ministries
P.O. Box 655 • Fenton, MO 63026

or call: (636) 349-0303

Internet Address: www.joycemeyer.org

In Canada, write: Joyce Meyer Ministries Canada, Inc.
Lambeth Box 1300 • London, ON N6P 1T5

or call: (636) 349-0303

In Australia, write: Joyce Meyer Ministries—Australia
Locked Bag 77 • Mansfield Delivery Centre
Queensland 4122

or call: (07) 3349 1200

In England, write: Joyce Meyer Ministries
P.O. Box 1549 • Windsor • SL4 1GT

or call: 01753 831102